O.K. I'm A Parent; Now What?

A Collection Of Articles About Mentoring, Modeling And Making Fantastic Families

Take your family from "This".....

.....to "This"

Brandi A. Davis

O.K. I'm A Parent, Now What?
Mentoring, Modeling And Making Fantastic Families

O.K. I'm A Parent; Now What?

A Collection Of Articles About Mentoring, Modeling And Making Fantastic Families

Brandi A. Davis

Copyright © 2011 Brandi A. Davis. All rights reserved.
Published by: DSI Press, Philadelphia Pennsylvania

No part of this book may be reproduced or transmitted in any form, or by any means, electronic or mechanical, including photocopying, recording, or by any information storage and retrieval system, without permission in writing from the author and publisher.

The scanning, uploading and distribution of this book via the internet or by any other means, without the permission of the author and publisher is illegal and punishable by law. Any attempt, to do so will be prosecuted to the fullest extent of applicable law.

Please purchase only authorized electronic additions, and please do not participate in or encourage electronic piracy of copyrighted materials. Your support of the authors rights is appreciated.

O.K. I'm A Parent, Now What?
Mentoring, Modeling And Making Fantastic Families

Special thanks to my family, Mom, Dad, Corey, Dan, and of course my love, Matt, who have always supported me on my journeys.

O.K. I'm A Parent, Now What?
Mentoring, Modeling And Making Fantastic Families

Brandi's Biography 9

Intro 11

Soothe Starting School Stress 13

The Chaos Calming Choosing Chip 17

GO TO SLEEP ALREADY!! 19

The View From Below..21

My Kids Never Listen 27

You Call This Kid Food? 33

Creating Kindly Kids 37

Getting Warmer..45

Snow-Days Used To Be Fun...................................49

A Twist On The Terrible Twos 53

"I Asked For A Bike Not A Baby" 57

Being Stuck 67

To Share Or Not To Share......................................69

Move Your Mornings..75

It's All Fun And Games..81

Time Out Is Over And Out 87

Accentuate The Positive...91

JUST GET DRESSED!!!!!! 93

When "CAUSE I SAID SO!" Is Not Enough 97

Positive Parenting Philosophies..................................105

Logical Consequences; A Parents Best Friend..........109

Recommended Reading...118

O.K. I'm A Parent, Now What?
Mentoring, Modeling And Making Fantastic Families

Brandi's Biography

Brandi Davis is a professional Parenting Coach with a Bachelors of Science in Child Development and Family Studies with 14 years of teaching experience. Brandi also lectures at multiple colleges and has been published in several local and national publications. Through personal coaching sessions, workshops, tele-classes, and Professional Development Classes for Teachers, Brandi explores with her clients proven solutions which are then tailored to specific family circumstances. *"What does YOUR ideal family look and feel like"*, is Brandi's first question. From there, Brandi guides parents, teachers and those who have children in their lives, on their own journey to realize their dream of a happy, loving, and cooperative family or classroom.

Your children will become what you are; so be what you want them to be.

David Bly

O.K. I'm A Parent, Now What?
Mentoring, Modeling And Making Fantastic Families

Intro

The world is changing and the "village" that our parents once had when we were growing up is rapidly disappearing. With transient jobs taking people cross-country, retiring parents moving to warmer climates, dual working parents, and longer working hours, parents are losing the time and helpers that our ancestors had. If you have a child in your life, you probably find yourself sometimes feeling a bit out to sea without a map to guide you. Here is this person, this child, whether it speaks or not, who has feelings, needs and ideas which, on a good occasion may differ from yours and on a bad occasion, can sabotage your day. Unfortunately there is this "us against them" feeling created between the child's world and the grown up, one which creates the battlefield that many adults find themselves on when dealing with their kids.

This book will help you find new ways to get what you need accomplished without all of the tantrums and power-struggles that create conflicts within the family. This book is a compilation of articles touching on a myriad of child rearing topics such as quick dinners, tantrums, how to get your kids to listen, stressless snow-days and more. This book covers parent-child communication, meal time tidbits, sibling prep work, ways to mentor kind kids, parent philosophies and much, much more. When you finish this book you will feel empowered to parent in a calmer, quieter and more productive way than you ever have before. Dive in and start your new parenting adventure now. Read the articles and take from them what fits into your family, then mold the concepts to fit your personality, your child's temperament, and your family ideals. Have fun and enjoy.

O.K. I'm A Parent, Now What?
Mentoring, Modeling And Making Fantastic Families

Article #1

Soothe Starting School Stress

Getting your children ready to go back to school

It is almost that time again. You know the one. The time to stick to schedules, time to wake up early, time to get out of the door on time. Ugh. It is BACK TO SCHOOL TIME!!!!!

Some children may have summer activities, camp, classes, daycare, but showing up late to those activities does not hold the same weight as showing up late to school. How can you be assured that you will be ready to get everywhere, with everyone, with everything that they need? Planning...Planning...Planning...

Ok, so lets make some plans:

PLAN #1

Figure out what time your team needs to be in the car driving away (or at the bus stop).

Not just heading to the car or bus stop, because that in itself is a process; Getting the bags, the lunches, turning lights off, locking the door, everyone in the car seat, making sure that you have everyone..... You need to know precisely how much time it takes from wake up to driving down the street or standing at the bus stop.

PLAN #2

Figure out what time everyone needs to wake up.

It takes no less than an hour to get a young child (or a teen for that matter) up, dressed, fed, and out of the door tantrum free. (Yes, even teens. Sub *attitude* for *tantrum*.) Most morning problems are caused by rushing. When tired children are rushed to get dressed, grab breakfast, and get out of the door, they go into sensory overload and head into tantrum land. Children need time. They need time to wake up, time to brush their teeth, time to get dressed, time to eat. Some children need A LOT of time to do these activities. Give them the time they need and it will pay off for you in the end. Grab a cup of coffee and the paper and you won't mind so much that it takes your kid 15 minutes to put on their underwear.

PLAN #3

Talk to your kids about getting everything ready for school before they hit the sack.

Starting a new school year is hard enough without adding battles about what your children are going to wear to school that day. The clothing war is one of the biggest wrenches thrown into a family's morning plan. Let your children pick out their clothes the night before. Consider using a fun phrase for younger kids "Pick out your clothes from your head to your toes", is a good mantra for young children. As long as it is weather appropriate and fits, do you really care what they look like? (Do you remember what we used to wear? Parachute pants. Oversized flannels. NEON!!!!! Need I say more?) That goes for lunch too. Have your children help you pack their lunch. If they are involved in the creating of their lunch they are more likely to eat it. If they think that a turkey and jelly sandwich is yummy, well, so be it. Kids with homework need to have it in their bag ready to go the night before. Stressful searches for homework are no way to start the day. Lunch made, clothes out, homework accounted for, and bags packed. Begin these routines the first week of school to start good habits and ensure a smooth school year.

PLAN #4

Practice getting up.

It can be a hard transition for some children to go from waking at 8 to waking at 6. Start waking your children up 15 minutes earlier in 2 week segments a few weeks before school starts. If they get up at 8 wake them at 7:45 for 2 weeks. Then 7:30 for 2 weeks. You can surely do whatever time line works for you, but a slow change can help children get acclimated to an earlier wake time in a smoother manner. Parents of children going to a new school (especially young ones going into kindergarten or first grade) may want to practice the whole routine the weekend before. Waking, breakfast, getting things together, and walking to where the bus will be. Talk through these activities as you do them so that your child knows what to expect. Even if the routine is the same as their pre school routine, go through it anyway. Children can forget the routine or may have trouble adjusting to new adventures, which can cause anxiety. The more informed and ready that your child is for the first day of school, the more effortlessly it will go. And the more effortlessly it goes for your children THE MORE EFFORTLESSLY IT GOES FOR YOU. Ahhh, a pleasantly uneventful first day of school. Perfect.

Too often we give children answers to remember rather than problems to solve.

Roger Lewin

Article #2
The Chaos Calming Choosing Chip

Field trips and out of the house adventures with kids are great experiences and essential on those rainy, freezing, or way too hot summer days. Oh, but how the fun can quickly evaporate when the fighting about what to do next arises.

"I wanna choose!!!"
"Its my turn!!!"
"I hate that part! It's for babies!!!"
(Feel free to insert your own family gripes here.)

Do you want to cut down on field trip fiascoes and fights? Who doesn't? One answer is a choosing chip. Or Wand. Or Coin. Or doll. Or..... You get the drift. Something small and easy to carry, which cannot be eaten by any toddlers. She/He who holds the choosing object gets to decide where in the zoo, museum or such, the team explores next. Decide the order of the choosers before you leave for the day. Oldest to youngest. Youngest to oldest. Draw straws. Whatever floats your boat, and feel free to put yourself in the line up, adults. You are part of the team and should have a choice too. No need to miss out on your favorites like the monkeys at the zoo or raptor fossils at a Dinosaur Museum. So go search your house for that great Choosing Chip. Better yet, have your kids make one. A round wood cut out from your local craft store, with a bit of paint and glitter.... Poof. Fabulous Choosing Chip! Now get out there and go have some fun.

O.K. I'm A Parent, Now What?
Mentoring, Modeling And Making Fantastic Families

Article #3
GO TO SLEEP ALREADY!!

Does your child leave their room at nap or bedtime? Are they calling for you instead of sleeping? Is your child spending more time fighting with you than resting? If this is your life, then read on. (If it's not your life, you should probably read on anyway. I mean ya did buy the whole book.)

The first thing to realize is that you cannot make someone sleep (unless you are going to use unsavory means and I'm *sure* that is not really the way that you want to handle this sleeping situation). So instead of making the goal to have your child sleep, make the goal be to have your child stay in their room and in their bed. If your child is in bed quietly reading, they are closer to sleeping than if they are fighting with you about nap or bedtime. At least if they are in bed chilling quietly they are resting and you have some "You Time."

Start by having a talk with your child;

"I know that sometimes you are not ready to sleep, but when it is time to go to your room, it is time to go to your room. You can listen to a book on tape or read if you like, but you need to stay in your room unless you have to go potty." Trust me, if your kid throws up or has a horrible nightmare they will let you know about it the moment it happens. You will not miss a thing.

Lets talk about morning, or almost morning, as some kids wake up at 5 A.M. and that still is considered night to many tired parents. Sometimes children wake up and come looking for you because they do not know what to do with themselves when they wake up. Make it clear to your child when they can leave their room. Have a light on a timer, a musical alarm or the like so that your child knows when they can open their door and start the day. Let them know that if they do get up they can read, or color or play quietly until the decided time. Better that they play quietly than wake you at 5 A.M., right?

Once the power struggles are left in the dust you will be surprised at just how quickly your child will end up falling asleep. This is really important to understand because many parents are afraid of this philosophy out of fear that their kids will stay up all night reading. It won't happen. Remember, us big people often read in order to make us more sleepy. You will also have children who are armed with a morning wake up plan that keeps them quiet and in their room until you are ready for them (assuming you do not sleep until noon). Now that is a dream come true for any parent.

Article #4
The View From Below
A Child's Play-By-Play Of The Holidays

It is the holiday season. I love it. Presents, cake, candy. It's the best. You what? Want me to wear what?

"But I hate that buttony shirt. It is too tight and the sweater is itchy. And... He's wearing it too?"

I hate looking like my brother!!!!! He is a baby.

"Where are we going?"

To grandma's. Oh that's the best. She always has cookies and toys and we can watch anything that we want. I will wear this itchy sweater for that.

Uh, who are all of these people?

I don't want to smile.

Get off.

I don't want a hug.

Ewww, who just kissed me?

"No I don't remember you."

Last year? Last year I was 2 and a half. How on earth am I gonna remember you with all of the other things that I am supposed to remember. Letters, numbers, colors, don't hit my brother, put the toys away when I am done, don't put that in my mouth, don't stand on the coffee table.... Really, like I am gonna remember you? Oh no. Not another kiss…… Now I have to go potty. Where's mommy, daddy?????? There are so many people here.

"Yes I am doing the potty dance Mr., Oh Uncle Al."

"Yes I have to go potty".

I did know where it was before all of you people showed up. Now its just legs and bottoms EVERYWHERE. Oh, thank goodness. Grandma will take me to the potty.

"OOOO, yeah I want a sneaky cookie before dinner".

Yes, I love this holiday. A present? For me?

"No I don't remember you from last year, I was…" Oh never mind. Ok, almost got it.

"I can do it myself".

A sweater. What is it with grown ups and itchy sweaters? I don't want to say thank you.

"Thank you."

I am not shy, I just don't have anything to say. Grown ups are boring. Why is that lady talking so slowly to me? Does someone need to change her batteries? That's what we did when my train started running too slow. No. She is talking to mommy like her batteries work. Huh? That guy is doing it too. Why do people always talk so slowly to me? I am 3 and a half. I am busy. I have places to go. Speed it up people.

"I am hungry."

Oh good dinner. Mmmmm, turkey, mashed potatoes. That was so good. Ok, now what?

"Can I go play?"

No? What am I waiting for? The grown ups need to stop talking. What is divorce and why is Aunt Patty getting that for the holidays? Do I want one?

Why is cousin Joe out of a job? We were out of milk the other day, we just bought more. Why doesn't someone buy him one so I can get up and PLAY?????

Finally they are getting up. Time to play.

Why, oh, why do these people keep asking me these questions?

"I am 3 and a half."

"Sure, everyone likes cookies."

"School is fine."

"A girlfriend? I am 3 and a half!!!!"

I am so tired.

"Mommy, is it time to go home yet?"

Almost? Phew. Ok, I can get ready. Put on my jacket. NO. No more kisses. I don't want a kiss goodbye. No, not you either.

"Can I kiss grandma good-bye?"

Ahhh and grandpa gives the best hugs. Made it. Car seat. Going home. Maybe next year those people will get lost, or be taken by aliens, or eaten by dinosaurs and it will be just us and grandma and grandpa. Now *that* would be *my* kind of holiday.

O.K. I'm A Parent, Now What?
Mentoring, Modeling And Making Fantastic Families

"Holding on to anger is like grasping a hot coal with the intent of throwing it at someone else; you are the one who gets burned."

Buddha

O.K. I'm A Parent, Now What?
Mentoring, Modeling And Making Fantastic Families

Article #5
My Kids Never Listen

Does this sound familiar? One of the most discussed topics on the playground, at lunch, or on parenting sites are children who just don't listen. Well, um, that is a VERY broad statement. Sure, sometimes your children are just tediously blocking you out, but more often then not there is a reason for a child's reluctance to comply with your demands or commands. Check out the following scenarios to find out why your child may not be responding to you and learn strategies and ideas that fit in with your family.

REASON ONE: YOUR KIDS ARE BUSY.

Though to you, your child is scribbling with crayons, stacking blocks, or listening to their ipod, to your child, these activities are much more meaningful. Those scribbles could represent something to your 3 year old, or your 7 year old may have been stacking those blocks for a half hour until they got it just right, or your child might just need some downtime with their music after 2 hours of studying for a midterm. When adults blow into a room, tell their kids to drop what they are doing to accommodate the parents needs, that sends a strong message. *I don't respect you or what you are doing. My needs are the important ones.* When children feel disrespected they use the greatest weapon that they have, **"NO!"** Once *that* battle begins the thing that you desperately needed done "right now", won't get done, or at least no where near the "right now" that you had intended. It also begins the battles of wills which leave both parties unhappy and disconnected.

THE SOLUTION: GIVE A HEADS UP AND RESPECT YOUR CHILD'S ACTIVITIES.

Walk into your child's situation with a semi flexible time line or choices (Unless of course it is an emergency. If someone needs a doctor run or needs to be picked up right away then all bets are off.) For example approach your child in the following way:

"Amy, I need to go to the market soon. I see that you are coloring/reading/watching a movie. Are you ready now or do you need 5 more minutes to find a place to pause or finish up?"

Children who are not yet used to this approach may still give you a bit of a hard time, but within a few encounters your exchanges will improve remarkably. In addition to giving choices on time, parents can offer a more portable toy choice for very young children to transition with or for older children, parents can ask if there is an errand that the child would like to run while you are all out. These approaches show your child that you respect their time and activities. It also models respectful interactions, and modeling and is the best way to teach children appropriate and positive behaviors.

REASON TWO: THEY DONT WANT TO...

Sometimes your kids just do not want to do the things that you ask. They do not want to eat dinner. They do not want to clean up. They do not want to put their shoes on or do their homework. They are flexing their autonomy muscles and just saying **"NO"**. Ok, now what? Screaming until you turn red is one choice. Tossing the shoes or homework across the room is another. Telling them that if they don't do what you say they will never eat candy again, go outside ever, or get into college is yet another strategy. Now, while some the previous strategies may be ones that you have tried before (happens to the best of us), they are not really all that productive in teaching your child to respect someone's words or needs.

THE SOLUTION: LOGICAL CONSEQUENCES AND TAKING RESPONSIBILITY FOR ACTIONS

Logical consequences are a part of our everyday lives. When we are late to work; we get reprimanded. When we procrastinate, we finish our work at night or on the weekend. Children and teens spend most of their time living in the moment. It is the job of the grown ups in their lives to teach them that their choices have consequences. For example, if your child refuses to clean up the activity that they are presently engaged in, then they cannot move onto anther activity. Honestly. If they sit in the middle of 42 Legos for an hour and a half in protest it is not affecting you, is it? Not nearly as much as yelling and screaming until you can feel the veins in your head popping out. *Your child* is the one missing the movie or family game time. What is important is to note that YOU are not punishing your child. Your child has the power to clean up and move on at any point. They are in control of their day and destiny. Another example is homework. If your child does not want to do their homework they will get a **"0"** on the assignment or miss something at school to finish the work not yet done. Often a teacher's discipline in these matters is more influential then a parents. Feel free to call the teacher and let them know that you are aware of the situation but would like your child to have a real world consequence for their actions. Your child is not going to miss out on going to Harvard because of one "0" on a 7th grade assignment. Taking responsibility for one's actions and logical consequences are some of the greatest teachers for the young *and* not so young.

REASON THREE: TIRED/HUNGRY/TIME OF DAY:

There are many grown ups who are bears when tired or hungry but we, at least, can express, suppress, or remedy the problem. Is your child always fighting with you at 11:30? Does your child tune you out at 2 P.M.? The reasons for the non-listening may be fixed simply when the causes are discovered.

SOLUTION: SWITCH THE SCHEDULE

Maybe lunch needs to be earlier or your child might need a bigger mid morning snack. Perhaps a nap or quiet time is in order. Even older kids need down time. Writing down when unpleasant episodes happen is a good way to figure out the catalyst of the tuning out or defiance. Often times children do not even know themselves why they are not feeling right, so asking them will not always help. That being said, no matter how hungry or tired someone is, they should not be given free reign to be argumentative and use words that are unkind. Explain to your child that we all feel grumpy, tired, or sad sometimes and there are many ways to express and cope with those feelings. They can use their words. They can draw a picture. They can find a quiet place to be. They can try to figure out the cause.... If you know that your child is hungry you can let them know that you will get them food as fast as you can, but speaking unkindly will NOT make the process move any quicker. No one deserves to be yelled at. Not even moms and dads.

So, now three major non-listening scenarios have been laid out with a few solutions. Feel free to use your own words or phrases that you feel more comfortable with. Remember that you are giving your children skills to last a lifetime. Listening, teamwork, and taking responsibility for one's actions are important life skills that can only be learned with opportunity and practice.

O.K. I'm A Parent, Now What?
Mentoring, Modeling And Making Fantastic Families

Article #6
You Call This Kid Food?

Hot dogs, greasy grilled cheese, pasta drowning in butter, chicken fingers... These are the foods labeled kid food? These foods are what comprise a kids menu or kids food? Who decided that? Shouldn't kid food be nutrition rich, protein packed, vitamin filled, food to help growing bodies, um, well, grow? Real food. Ya know. The food that is NOT made in a lab or does not contain ingredients with 28 letters. The idea that grilled chicken, whole wheat pasta with vegetables, and turkey sandwiches are not kids food is preposterous. Growing bodies need nutrients not grease, fake food, and fat. So what to do? **Just do not buy it.** Do not have chicken fingers in your house, or pizza bites, or fish sticks. Make your own grilled chicken fingers. Have a "Make your own pizza night" with a pizza bar full of real and fresh ingredients. Bake your own home made fish sticks.

As we all know eating at home is not always an option and a night out to dinner can be a fun excursion. When you do venture out with your family, order healthier items off of the menu. Steer clear of the "Children's Menu" and focus on the "Grown Up Menu" where there are more fresh options to choose from.

As your children grow into eating solid foods, do not start them on processed foods. If children are not exposed to processed and fat filled foods they will not eat or crave them. Do not fall prey to fast food or frozen foods speed, or your friend's pressures about saving time, or a title given on a menu. If you have "Kid's Food" in your home, get it out. Your family can begin healthy eating anytime. It is never too late. Oh, and healthy eating habits do include treats here and there. Enjoy some ice cream, take out pizza, a burger, a cookie, or some pie from time to time with your kids. Treats are great. But when it comes to daily meal times, the food should be of the healthy, muscle building varieties. Give it a try. Your future grown up kids will thank you.

As adults, we must ask more of our children than they know how to ask of themselves. What can we do to foster their openhearted hopefulness, engage their need to collaborate, be an incentive to utilize their natural competency and compassion...show them ways they can connect, reach out, weave themselves into the web of relationships that is called community.

Dawna Markova

O.K. I'm A Parent, Now What?
Mentoring, Modeling And Making Fantastic Families

Article #7
Creating Kindly Kids

Good kids, they're what all parents want, right? Let's first delve into what, in the context of *this* article, is meant by "GOOD KIDS."

Good Kids:

Good kids listen because they know it is important to hear what others say. Good kids do what is asked, because they know that helping others is an essential piece of the societal puzzle. Good kids are kind, because kindness rewards them with kindness and because it feels good to help others and be a part of a team. Good kids take responsibility for their world, whether it is cleaning up a mess, doing homework, or apologizing for a step in the wrong direction. Good kids understand that they are a part of a larger tribe of family, friends, and community. Good kids express their emotions in productive ways. They will cry when sad or frustrated and tell you when they are confused or angry with calm, constructive words. Good kids will be happy and excited while using inside voices, keep their feet on the floor and hands to themselves when kindly asked to. (What this means is that your kids will not scream at you, have overwhelming tantrums, and/or run around your house bouncing on the furniture.) Good kids do good because it feels good. Good kids do not do "good" out of fear of punishment or because they are made to.

O.K. I'm A Parent, Now What?
Mentoring, Modeling And Making Fantastic Families

Sound kinda heavy? A bit much for your 3 year old to get? Think your 15 year old will never be that "good"? The words are big and meaningful. Maybe your kids will be resistant at first to calmly expressing their feelings or sticking around to hear you calmly express yours. Sure, your kids may not understand that the above reasons are why they are doing what they are doing, but it *is* why. So how do you create these super kids? I'll let you know. One thing though, remember kids are people just like you and I, and I can guarantee that you and I are not ALWAYS pleasant, kind, helpful, and "good", so do not expect more of your children than you yourself can do. Let's jump right in.

Kids Who Listen, Hear, And Respond To What Others Say.

Why do we listen to others? Hmm, twist that actually into why *don't* we listen? Yes, I mean you. Why don't *you* listen to someone (boss, friend, partner, family)? Often times we shut down around folks who do not make us feel respected. If your boss is always mistreating you, or your partner is using less then kind words, you may not do what they ask or you may fight back or you may take your time to respond to their needs. If you want your kids to do what you ask them to do, you need to begin by building a relationship founded on mutual respect and kindness.

For example, YOU may want to go to the market right now but your kid might have had other plans. Perhaps your 3 year old is working on a Lego town or your 13 year old is in the middle of homework, or your teen is heading out to their friends house and does not want to baby sit. These are all very valid reasons not to want to jump at your request. It is not that you will now, in your quest for a reciprocally respectful relationship, be unable to go to the market, but you will have to realize that you are now imposing on your child. And no, your kids are not imposing on you when you need to make dinner for them or drive them to school. That is the responsibility that came along with the job that you signed up for when you entered into parenthood. If you are going to need something from your children, give a heads up or update. Let your three year old know that you need to hit the market and that you would like to leave in five or ten minutes. Ask them which they would rather do and of course they can save what they are working on so they can finish their project later. Asking them to clean up and run out of the door within 10 minutes is sure to spark a fire that you most likely will not be able to quickly put out. Perhaps let them bring a few Legos in the car to work on so that they do not have to completely give up their playtime. Warnings are important for older kids too; As are specifics. Let your kids know how long you will need them for so that they can plan their day accordingly. Perhaps for the babysitting teen you can make a stop for something that they need OR hurry home and NOT prolong your errands. Also feel free to lavish your kids with thanks when they do hop aboard your plan, even if it *is* with a bit of reluctance. You will be surprised on the day when your child says; "Thanks for making dinner" or mumbles; "Thanks for the ride." You will also see your kids needing less and less warnings and will begin to be quick to help because they do not feel the need to make a point of pushing back to demonstrate that you can't boss them around. If you make your children's work and world a priority, you will find that they will be more willing to do the same for you.

Kids Who Express Themselves Purposefully

Children, just like us grown ups, have a variety of feelings, such as anger, happiness, frustration, disappointment, excitement... And just like us grown ups, children do not always express those feelings in the most productive way. Perhaps a child's excitement is being expressed in a yelling voice or running feet. Anger might come out as a tantrum, or frustration might cause hitting hands or less than respectful words. So how can parents allow for feelings and the expression of them, but still keep some sense of calm in their home? Teach your children by modeling and mentoring, how to express their feelings and needs. Change your child's:

"PUT MY SHIRT ON NOW!" Into "Can you help me with my shirt please?"

"NO!" Into "Can I finish this one part and then clean up the rest?"

"MOMMY STAY. I SAID STAY. NO. DON'T GO TO WORK!" Into "I miss you when you go to work."

How To Get Kids Who Express Themselves Purposefully

Acknowledge Child: Stop what you are doing, look at them and let the child know that you are listening. In time they will do the same for you.

Identify Emotion: By identifying the emotion you are also saying, "I'm listening to you and you matter." It also helps children recognize what they are feeling and be able to name it. When children understand their feelings, they can react and soothe themselves productively. Eg, "You sound angry." "You seem frustrated." " You look very proud."

Give Room For Child To Talk: Children will talk more when grown ups talk less. Do not be afraid of a little silence. Resist the urge to jump in and solve, make better, or discipline.

Support Child's Problem Solving: Ask the child how they can fix their situation. Adults may have to help a little here.

"You are saying that you are frustrated with that puzzle, what would make you enjoy the puzzle more (make you feel better...)" The child might want you to help, have a friend or sibling help, walk away for a bit.... All wonderful solutions.

When children learn how to face and solve their problems, their feelings, while still there, are diffused a bit. They know that while they are frustrated or upset, there is something that they can do about it.

Put It Together: Looking at the child and at their level. "Amy you look like you are getting upset." "Oh so what I am hearing is that you were playing with the blocks and Bill walked by and knocked them down. That would be upsetting. What do you think that you can do to make yourself feel better?" "Yes, you can tell him to try to be more careful when he is walking. Let's go do that now." "Amy, you expressed your feelings positively while letting Bill know that you were upset. How do you feel now?" Don't forget to model what you are expecting from your children. When you are upset identify your own emotions and express them calmly and clearly. Be what you want your children to become and they will do so.

Kids Who Are Kind

Being a kind person goes beyond being nice or good. A kind person is considerate, helpful, tolerant and understanding. How do we, as adults, instill these qualities in the children in our care? Well, first of all we, ourselves, must be kind. We must model forgiveness, understanding, consideration, and the like. We must treat children, peers, family, and significant others with kindness. We must expect kindness and mentor how to be kind.

Examples of how to mentor kindness...

Have children take responsibilities for their actions instead of making them say "I'm Sorry." If Sam knocks over Ben's blocks, Sam then asks Ben how he can fix the situation that he has created. Sam also asks Ben how he can make Ben feel better. Maybe Sam will need to fix what was broken. Give Ben more space. Whatever Ben needs. If Ann hurts Ella, Ann asks Ella what she can do to make it better, even if it was an accident. Ann could sit next to Ella, get ice, give a hug. There is also the possibility that the offended party may say that there is nothing that will make them feel better right now and that is O.K.. Sometimes we are so hurt or upset that others cannot fix the situation. In the previous scenarios, the children had to help remedy the situation that was caused, even if it was an accident. They become part of the solution and can see and fix the affects of their action, as opposed to muttering "sorry" and leaving the scene. Forcing a child to say sorry is not actually having them take responsibility for their actions AND you may be putting them in a position to lie. They may *not* be sorry. They may have been mad and *meant* to knock the blocks over, so insisting on a sorry is insisting that the child lie.

When a child has helped you or someone else, make a point to notice and acknowledge it. Thank a child for noticing your happy or not so happy mood. Make note to a child when you have seen them help a friend who has tripped. They will learn that they are on the right track and continue to make the kind and caring choices like those that you witnessed.

Model kindness yourself. Be helpful to the children in your life. Help a child clean a very messy room. Make right when you wrong them. If you yelled too loud or got angry about something that a child did not do, apologize. You will not lose a speck of authority, but you WILL gain a mountain of respect.

Kids Who Understand That They Are One Part Of A Community

Children can only understand that they are a part of a community when they are treated that way. If children live in a segregated world, one where two groups exist: one Grown Up group and one Kid group, they will not understand what it is to be a part of a larger community. They will see that friction and division are the norm. They will *not* learn that what they do affects the group both positively and negatively. They will *not* see how much they are worth as part of that community. They will *not* see how helpful, funny, or inventive they are. (and yes I am talking about your 2, 3 , 4, 7, 10, 14, 17 year old.) When one understands and internalizes the idea that they are a part of a community, they grow compassion, understanding, patience, tolerance, foresight, helpfulness and kindness; All attributes that bode well for your family, the community, and your child's future.

How do you create kindly kids? Create a kindly home. Surround yourself with kindly people. Parent and mentor in kindly ways and expect kindly behavior. That is how you create kindly kids.

Article #8
Getting Warmer
An action plan to support your "slow to warm" child

"Don't be outgoing today." "Don't be cheerful and upbeat at the party." "Don't bring your funny, witty self to dinner." WHAT???? That sounds ridiculous doesn't it? You would never say that to your child. Oh, but the opposite has been muttered many, many times:

- *"Don't bring your quiet self to thanksgiving dinner."*
- *"Leave your shy self at home when we see our friends tonight."*
- *"If you don't play with your friends at the party today we are going home."*

Yes, it would be great if we were all cheerfully tempered and outgoing people, but not everyone is made that way. Some take a little longer to feel comfortable in situations; even with people that they see everyday. Some people are just quieter than others. Do you know anyone like that? A friend? A family member? You?

Many parents are using the term "Shy" (often with a tone indicating shame, embarrassment or disapproval) to describe their children, and kids hear and feel that. Shy is a label with many negative connotations, and in many cases is inaccurate. Shyness can be a more extreme condition which may result in anxiety, avoidance of social situations, or interfere with the enjoyment of activities. If your child is the one who needs to stay with a parent for a little while before they go and play. The one that will watch from the back for a bit before joining in. The one who needs time before they will say "Hi". Your child is more *"slow to warm"* than shy. *"Slow to warm"* children need time to suss out a situation, time to take it all in, but **will**, eventually join in the fun, start talking, and may even become an outgoing and loud member of the group. Research, as documented by Elaine Aron in her book <u>The Highly Sensitive Child</u>, has shown that "slow to warm" children take in more sensory information (sounds, sights, smells....,) which increases the likelihood that they will become overwhelmed more easily than children who are not "slow to warm." "Slow to warm" children need time to soak it all in and process the abundance of information running into their eyes, ears, and nose before they wade into situations. Other kids just jump in. Neither child's approach is better or worse. It just is. It is their temperament. It is who they are.

So now what? Are you destined to have to endure your child clinging to your leg for a half hour at every party or function? No. No you do not. It is important to respect who your child is and their temperament, but you can coach and help them feel more comfortable about going into new situations.

- Tell your child where you are all going the night before. Give them as much information as you have. (The place, theme, food, people...)
- Let your child know that it is o.k. to need some time before talking.

- Let them know that many children and grownups feel the same way as they do.
- Bring them into the process of comforting themselves. "I know birthday parties are not easy for you at first. What would make you feel more comfortable?"
  - Maybe carpool with a friend so they walk in with someone.
  - Plan to meet a friend at the door.
  - Come early so that your child has time to take in the surroundings.
  - Let them hold your hand or sit next to you. (It is your body and if you do not want your child hanging on you, you do not have to let them. They need security, and your hand will do just fine.)
- See if they can start slow. If someone says "Hi", request a wave or smile from your child.
- Do not be embarrassed. If someone gets upset or is pushing to have your child talk, tell them plainly that your wonderful child just arrived and when she is ready she will start conversing with people.
- Pushing will only make it worse. It will only make your child feel that there is something wrong with them and will make them more nervous.
- Keep labels off of your child. When people label children as mean, they will become that role. When people label their children as lazy, they will slide into laziness. If you label your child as shy, they will think it

is who they are and stay there. Labels are sticky and hard to remove.

You may be the parent, but your kids are whole and complete people of their own. They have their own thoughts, feelings and personalities. It is not our job as grown ups to fix children or mold them into what we want them to be. We are there to guide them through choices and situations. If your child is outgoing, that is wonderful. They may need to learn to give others some space to talk and play and that is just fine. If your child is "slow to warm", they may need to learn skills to prepare themselves for new or crowded situations, and skills on how to comfort themselves when they get there. THAT is your job.

Abraham Lincoln, Albert Einstein, Thomas Edison, Eleanor Roosevelt, Mia Hamm. What do they all have in common? They were once labeled as shy, and look what they became.

O.K. I'm A Parent, Now What?
Mentoring, Modeling And Making Fantastic Families

Article #9
Snow-Days Used To Be Fun....

Ahhhhh, remember when snow days meant sledding, snowball fights, hot chocolate, and FUN? Unfortunately as grownups it is more about shoveling, salting and kids home from school. Do not give up. Snow days can be almost as fun as they used to be. Yes, almost, don't want to get the hopes up *too* high. Here are some thoughts and ideas:

1. You do not have to play with your kids for the next 24-48 hours. Dump some blocks of the floor, put out puzzles, tell your kids to play, and YOU go have some "YOU time."
2. You do not have to be cruise director of your house. Every moment does not have to be filled with an organized activity. *"First we build snowmen. Then inside for cocoa. Then we cut snowflakes and glue them. Then we build an igloo out of boxes inside. Then it's back outside and...."*
3. You think 30 minutes of T.V. a day is enough? Well maybe on a snow day you can break that rule. How far can you get in your book, or how long a nap can you take, or how many people can you check on Facebook during that time. Ahhhh...
4. Tell your kids what's going on and have them ready activities that they would like to do on their snow day. That way they will have toys and fun already out, and

YOU do not have to spend the day finding the next activity for your kids to do.
5. Find activities that you *would enjoy* doing with your kids. Relish the extra bit of family time that you are getting treated to.
6. Remember a snow day is like a vacation day. Relax, bend some rules, give your kids space (yes they do want it, even if it does not seem that way), and have a good time.

O.K. I'm A Parent, Now What?
Mentoring, Modeling And Making Fantastic Families

All children behave as well as they are treated.

Jan Hunt

O.K. I'm A Parent, Now What?
Mentoring, Modeling And Making Fantastic Families

Article #10
A Twist On The Terrible Twos

Just because your child has turned two and has ideas of their own, (oh and they express said ideas through, screaming, hitting or kicking), does not mean that your sweet baby is now gone forever. There are ways to quell the chaos of the Tenacious (note, not TERRIBLE) Twos.

The first thing to remember about two year olds is that there is a LOT going on in their minds and not nearly enough ways for them to express it all verbally. You do not understand what they are so clearly (so they think) expressing, and this is often the catalyst for your child's anger at you. Like when they shove that kid who will not get away from them while playing at the park.

The other piece of the puzzle is that they have not yet learned how to act and react in social situations. We are not born knowing how to wait a turn or not to shove someone when they have something that we want. Quite the opposite. Do not forget that at the core of it all, we are animals and animals use force to get what they want or when they are mad. Your child is going to have to learn how to behave in this society of ours and the education starts with you.

To your children you are the model of humanity. What you do, they will do. If you wait your turn, say excuse me and please, so will your children. If you yell or grab, you guessed it, so will your kids.

That being said, here are a few quick hints on how to handle those times when your child's lack of social intelligence shines through. Always think *"Life Lesson"* over *"Punishment"*

- Repeat, repeat, repeat the rules. If you are going to the playground, repeat the rules. If you go to dinner, repeat the rules. If you go to grandmas, repeat the rules. Whatever your rules are, repeat them over and over and over again. Do not assume your child remembers them even if you just said them yesterday.

- When your child hits or kicks, give words to use instead of their body. "Say back up please," or "Say excuse me please," or "using that"...then tell her that if she hurts another person she will have to sit down and not play. I am not a fan of the use of the words "Time Out". They have just been turned into another way to say you are bad and you are in trouble. Adults tend to just tell children that they are in "Time Out" but fail to actually discuss the offense at hand or why a time out is the best course of action.

- If he does it a second time lead him (or take him) to a quiet place to sit. Again telling him "you chose to hit, kick, push... someone and that is not safe. You need to take a break from playing until you can be safe. The playground, home, restaurant... is for all of us and until you can use your words (little that they may be) you will not be able to....."(insert what they were doing at that moment. Play, sit at the table, watch a movie.) No, your child will not get all of the words but over time they will understand. By the way, use big words with your child and they will learn big words. Only use small words with your child and they will only learn small words. If they still won't sit or they throw a big freak out, then it is time to go home. (Sure, you can sit and wait out a mini-mad fit. Most parents have been there and who cares if they look?)

- When it is time for your child to re-enter the activity (have them only sit for a minute or two) let your child know that if they hurt someone again that you are going to take them home, remove them from that area, or end the activity that is causing the aggression.

This will not be fun, but the sooner you start these life lessons, the sooner the unwanted behavior stops. The point is for your child to understand that hurting is not O.K. and if she/he hurts, she/he cannot be with people because it is not O.K. to hurt those around us. Also your child is a part of something larger then just themselves. They are a part of a community. The idea of community and a persons place in the community is a lesson that takes time to learn. There are folks who, even as adults, still have not fully learned the lesson of community.

LAST THOUGHT:

ONCE YOU SAY IT, DO IT! If you say that your child can't slide if they do *xyz*, or "We will have to go home if you do *lmnop*." STICK WITH IT! DO NOT SAY SOMETHING THAT YOU ARE NOT GOING TO DO. If you are not going to go home, don't say that. If you are not going to take away movie night, don't say that you will. With consistency, clear rules and a calm head you can transform the Terrible Twos.

Article #11
"I Asked For A Bike Not A Baby"

Your vision of family might be a bunch, or a few, or 2 kids running around laughing, playing, going to the park, vacations, lovely breakfasts, holidays. Ahhhh. Your child's idea of family is, um, well... EXACTLY HOW IT IS NOW!!!!!! While a new baby is often a gift, a welcome or much desired addition for a parent; To the child that is presently living with you, it may not be such a festive treat. Your child probably likes the way things are now and they will be quick to notice how the family starts to change once a new baby's arrival gets announced. Maybe mommy is sick or tired. There may be lots of talk about things to come or what needs to be bought for the new baby leaving the "Old Baby" possibly feeling a bit left out.

Your child might be thinking.

"I am right here. You can buy things for me! I need things,"

So what can parents do to soften the blow of the impending arrival of a new sibling? First of all, realize that changing the family dynamic can be extremely traumatic to a child. Their life has been lived one way and now it is changing. Change is HARD! You know it. I know it. Kids know it. Second, try to see it this way: *If you have a cupcake and you are asked to share half with someone else, you now have less cupcake.* A child can see love in this way too, as something that is limited. There is only so much to go around and if a new baby comes they will take some of that parent love and leave less for child #1. We, as grownups, know that love is limitless, but remember kids are not grown ups and cannot be reasoned into seeing things the way that we see them. So now what? Are you doomed to feelings of guilt and exhaustion trying to create a perfect family transition? NO WAY. It will be difficult, but there are a few things that you can do to make the transition to a bigger family go a bit more smoothly.

There is a lot to do when a new baby is on the way; Like getting the baby furniture back out or acquiring new items, decorating the room, buying clothes, thinking of names. No need to leave your child out of it all. Enlist their help in picking out the decor or colors or name. By the way, just because your child makes a suggestion does not mean that you must use it. You do not have to name your baby Elmo and have a green, orange, and black polka dot room because your child came up with that, oh so, creative suggestion. Pick one color that they chose and perhaps find a blanket, doll, or picture using said color. You can put their baby name choices on a list. A child could also create art to hang in the babies room. Just including a child can make them feel that the baby is a family event not a mommy and daddy event.

The crib, blanket, high chair, toy; Did they at one time belong to child #1? Unwittingly, parents tend to overlook, how a child feels when their belongings are being used by someone else. A child might have grown out of the object, but it is still theirs and the child may be very upset when it is given away to someone else to use. Yes, even if they have not looked at or used it in forever. Just ask permission to use your child's things for the baby. (You may have bought the crib or chair or blanket but *they* have been using it for the past few years.)

As the big day gets closer, be sure to share the plan of action with your child/children. Some plans to express could be:

• Where will your child stay while you are giving birth?

• Will they continue to go to school while you are giving birth and recovering?

• Will they have the food that they like where they are staying? (Yes, that is REALLY important.)

• Will your child be able to bring comfort items to where they will be staying?

• Let them know what things will be the same while the baby is being born. Teachers, lunches, school trips, books to be read.....

The more information that you give to your child about the birthing day and the like (not information about you necessarily, but more about your child and their world) the more comfortable he/she will be while you are away and in the days leading up to the birth.

"Don't hug the baby so hard. Don't feed the baby that. Babies can't do that. STOP!" After a baby is born, kids find that there are a lot of new rules that they are expected to know, even if they had not been told yet what they are. Before the baby joins the family let your child/children know what they can do with the newborn, which at first thought may not seem like a whole lot. Notice parents, I said tell your kids what they *CAN* do, NOT what they *CAN'T* do with the baby. *"DON'T DO"s* are confusing. Ok so your child cannot hit, or bite, or play ball with, or squeeze too hard (whatever that means), or..... It might be difficult, but find things that the younger folks in the house CAN do with the new bundle. For example they can touch softly with 2 fingers, they can kiss on the hand, foot, or top of the head. They can read to the baby, color "with" the baby. They can pick clothes out for the baby, because as big kids they are really good at picking out clothes (mismatch clothing is a worthy sacrifice for family harmony). They can tell the baby funny family stories, or traditions, or help feed. There are many things that can be done with the baby.

"Nothing will change honey. Everything will be the same. There will be just more of us to love and to love you. It will be great." You know that the previous statement sounds good, and it sounds just like what a parent should say, and it sounds so wonderfully reassuring, and IT IS A BIG FAT LIE!!! Oh, and when your kid finds out that you have lied, you will be in a world of trouble. They will be angry in ways that you do not want to think that your sweet angel could be angry. And they will let you know just how mad that they are. So what to do?? *Tell your kids that you will be so tired and things will totally suck for them like it did for you (maybe) when your little sister or brother came and no one talked to you anymore and you had to give away all of your old things and....???* Well, sort of. Kids are tougher than we think that they are and they do, in the long run, appreciate the honesty. Do not wait expectantly for a "Thank you for your honesty parents" or flowers. What you will get is a kid ready for what is really to come and your thanks will be in the form of fewer tantrums. Let your child know that you will be tired and that you may have a little less time to do the things that they may want to do. You might be really busy because babies cannot do anything for themselves. Let your child know that babies can be loud and do not make great playmates at first because they cannot do all that much in the beginning. Reassure them that you will love them just as much as you do right now. Let your child know that if they are feeling left out they can come and talk to you about it. They can tell you any feelings that they are having. You may not want to hear all that they have to say about the baby, but do it anyway.

Maybe your friends have told you, or you have seen it first hand, perhaps a teacher at your child's school gave you the heads up. What could I be speaking of? REGRESSION! The bedwetting, passy wanting, whining, crying, crawling, and baby talk. Your "big kid" begins to turn into a baby. It can drive a parent batty. So why are these kids doing these insane things? Kids are smart. They do what they have to do in order to get what they need. If that means using kind words, helping out, throwing a tantrum, making wrong choices, or acting like the new baby, well they will try it. Jump into your child's tiny shoes and see the situation from their view. *This new THING that can't do anything, and cries, and poos, and crawls, is what everyone is cooing over. While everyone used to get so excited by each of my independent milestones, now they just take them for granted and expect even more. It's not fun to be big. No one likes you anymore. They only like that helpless, oozing, crying THING. What happened to me being the baby? That was only like 9 or so months ago when everyone was still fawning all over me, telling me how cute I am.* Hmmm. Interesting, right? So what would you do if you were wearin' those tiny shoes? **Act like the attention getting, crying, helpless, oozing, tiny *THING* right**? I would. So are you doomed to now have 2 infants? NO WAY! First of all, ignore what you can.

"But my kid is making me crazy with all of the crawling and whining." You say.

Though it is hard to believe (and I have not mastered this 100% either) *we* control our reactions to things. Now, I am not talking about major life catastrophes, but the smaller everyday annoyances that come along. That rude bank teller, your boss forgetting your name AGAIN, your significant other doing that thing that drives you nuts, your 5 year old acting like an infant... Take a breath and remember that you do not have to be bothered. Try to ignore the behavior and even leave the room. If a behavior does not get the desired effect, your child will move onto another plan.

There is nothing wrong with having your child take responsibility for themselves and their actions. There are a lot of life lessons to be learned when we have to clean up the messes that we make. If your child begins to have accidents all of a sudden (the wetting ones, not the poopy ones) have them find new clothes and change themselves. No need to get angry. Remember, anger and yelling are forms of attention and embarrassing or belittling your child are never good ways to get a message across. Help with what they cannot do such as buttons and zippers and then go on with the day without mention of it. Perhaps, up the number of times there is a bathroom break in the day. If its the whining that gets your goat, simply tell your child that you do not understand what they are trying to communicate and that you are truly interested and will be ready to hear what they have to say when they can use a calmer, more quiet voice. You can also acknowledge the behavior head on "It seems like it would be fun to be a baby again, huh?" See where your child then takes you. See what they have to say. Perhaps they need to talk some feelings out. You know your child. Pick what you feel works best and if plan A does not work, try something else. Your child will also appreciate their new grown up role if being older was more enticing. Give some "big kid" privileges such as a later bedtime, 15 minutes will not hurt much, but it will make a world of difference to your child. Regression.... Fun stuff.

"I hate the baby. I am going to throw it away and everything will be just like it was before."

This sounds like a very frightening statement, does it not? Well unless your child has a history of extreme violence, you really do not have too much to worry about. Think about how many times you have said that you were going to "kill" someone or "kick the @#$% out of someone." You didn't really do it, nor would you have. You were just really upset. So is your kid. Things were going just fine for them and then WHAM, their world changes. Your child might have a variety of feelings and they may all show up on the same day. They may love the baby and think it's cute. Then they may be sad and miss those times when you could just up and head to the park. Then they may get mad because the baby won't stop crying and you won't put the movie in that they want or read a book to them. The one thing to keep in mind is that punishment does not make the anger go away, it just makes the child push it down deeper and get angry at you for not understanding. So what can you do when your child is getting angry about the baby? Just listen. There is no need to talk, just listen. Let them know that you will be there for them; that you will listen to what they have to say and that you want to hear about what they are feeling. Let them draw a picture focusing on how they feel. Tell them to run as fast as they are upset. Let your child know that you are hearing them, "You don't like the baby right now." "You feel left out." "You sound sad." I know that I do not like when people tell me what not to feel. "I hate Amy. I can't believe she did that." "Oh you don't hate Amy. She has been your best friend since college." I don't want to hear that. Likely neither does your child. Children need a chance to vent, just as we big people do.

A few bits and pieces to help you get through this time:

- Your child does not care if "Ben" is a great big brother and that you want them to be more like "Ben."

- Your child does not sympathize with your exhaustion so do not expect them too. "Babies are a lot of work. We are so very tired so we can't play with you." Your child is not old enough to think outside of themselves and empathize with what you are feeling. Do not make that an expectation of yours.

- Give definites. "When I am done feeding the baby I will read to you." "In 10 minutes I will be ready to play."

- Get help from friends and family. Have them take the baby so that your "big-kid" gets their time or have them take your "big-kid" out to do something special.

- Do not forget through the pregnancy and new babydom that your "big-kid" has class trips, plays, birthday parties, sporting events, and the like. It is easy to forget the every day stuff when the house is adjusting to someone new, but those activities are important to your "big-kid".

Many of us have survived being the big sibling and your children will too. The key to survival is understanding that having a baby is a huge life event. It is to you and it is to your child. Navigating through this change involves acknowledging that your perspective as *parents wanting to expand your family*, may differ from a smaller and younger member who might be just fine with the status quo. You may get very involved in the upcoming event and the new life that a baby brings, but try to remind yourself that there is another person who lives in the house who still has softball, and art class, and ballet. Another person who used to be the center of attention and now has to share the spotlight. A person who was not consulted (not that they should be) on this momentous family change. Your child is going through a large adjustment and they have no idea what is going to happen next. That's difficult for us as adults to deal with imagine it at 3, 4, 5, 6....

O.K. I'm A Parent, Now What?
Mentoring, Modeling And Making Fantastic Families

Article #12
Being Stuck

Do you find yourself yelling at your kids, while your blood pressure rises because they won't listen? You just want them to clean up their toys, go potty, put dishes in the sink, get dressed... I mean really, put the shoes on, clean your toys, WHAT'S THE BIG DEAL?!?!?!?!?!?!? O.k., here is the quick solution and it only involves one idea **Being Stuck**. When your child, for example, will not put their shoes on, they are **stuck**. When your child refuses to clean up, they are **stuck**. When your child won't brush their teeth, they are stuck. What that means is that until they can complete the task at hand, they cannot move on to another activity. Your child refuses to take a bath? They are stuck. They cannot move on to another activity until they bathe. There is no need to yell, fight or bribe. You state what's going on; "Until you take a bath (clean up, put shoes on...), you are stuck. You cannot move on to another activity until you have finished this one. When you have taken your bath and get unstuck you may play with something else (go outside, watch a movie.....), but until then you are stuck. You are in control of your day/evening and you can get yourself UNstuck anytime that you want to."

Grab a book if you want to, go get some things done if you can. Your child will quickly realize that you mean business. The life lesson? You are responsible for your actions. You make a mess, you clean it up. You do not put your shoes on, you can not go to the park. You do not put your dishes in the sink, you cannot come to family T.V. time. Parents, your reward is the calm feeling of not having to yell and fight. Hey, we have all been stuck at one point or another. It's all a part of life and learning what it means to be a part of a community.

Article #13
To Share Or Not To Share
That Is The Question

"He has all of the blocks. I want some." "She is using all of the cars. When's it my turn?"

How do you handle these types of situations? Do you take blocks away from a child who has been working, oh so, diligently for a half an hour already, with a clear plan of the desired result? Yup, you read that right, ***working***. Should the work of a child who is trying to create something that has been thought through from start to finish be sacrificed? Hmm, let's see what you think.

Time and time again parents are told to teach children the importance of sharing. As valuable as this lesson of sharing can be, so is instilling the sense of pride in one's work, and a sense that a persons endeavors are important and respected.

Let's put this in grown up terms. If you are playing solitaire and your spouse asks for some of your cards, are you required to give them up? How would you finish your game without all of the cards? What if you are reading a book and someone else around you wants to read a book. Must you give them the book? Is that not the same scenario as when grown ups ask a child to share blocks, cars, and other toys when they are in the middle of solo play?

There is also a harsh reality that some parents do not like to think of. Often times, a child only wants another child's toy because the other child has it. I can hear the gasps now. "Oh no. Not my child." *Oh yes, my friend, your child*. If those blocks or books or such were just there on the floor or in a box, they would not be nearly as alluring as when they are in the hands of another child.

Does this mean that sharing should never be encouraged? Should adults let their children hoard toys all of the time? Oh no, no, no. Children need to learn to share. (You have met those grown ups that never learned that lesson, right? Yikes.) Children need to learn, as grown ups do, that they are a part of a larger community and all does not belong to them because they see it, touch it, or want it.

It is possible to promote sharing *and also* respect solo play:

Sharing can be promoted at the beginning of an activity. When two children are headed to play with blocks at the same time, that is a great opportunity to educate them about sharing. Ask them how they would like to divide up the blocks? Are they building together? Or you can simply let them play and point out positive sharing moments to reinforce the wonderful sharing behavior.

Sharing can be promoted when a child is in the middle of a solitary activity. An adult (or a child) can ask if the engaged child would like to share. Maybe one child can build a garage, while another builds a house. Perhaps one child could wash the cars and the other parks them. You get the gist.

Another way to see sharing through a child's eyes is this: When a toy is being shared, one child has gained something while the other has lost something. Many times when a new child arrives into a situation, the playing child is asked to involve the newcomer and share their toys. If Amy is building a stable to hold her horses out of blocks and she is asked to share, how does it feel from Amy's point of view? She had to hand over her materials from her project to give them to someone else. When was the last time you walked into someone's home who was knitting and their significant other took some of their yarn and gave it to you? You would think that was weird. The knitter was in the middle of something and now he/she will not be able to finish. Yet many adults have such disregard for the work of a young child.

So, you have reached the end and may be thinking, Now what??? Do I make my kid share or not??? Ahhh, well like everything in life, sharing is not a black and white situation. Each situation is as different, as is each child. Keep in mind that *sharing* is equally as important a lesson as is *respecting the work of another*. The next time that you find yourself in the familiar situation of *to share or not to share*, see which lesson best applies. Parenting is not about finding the absolute answer. It is about finding enough tools for your tool belt, so that when your next project arises the tools are there for you to choose from.

O.K. I'm A Parent, Now What?
Mentoring, Modeling And Making Fantastic Families

O.K. I'm A Parent, Now What?
Mentoring, Modeling And Making Fantastic Families

Children are not our property, and they are not ours to control any more that we were our parents' property or theirs to control.

Richard Bach

O.K. I'm A Parent, Now What?
Mentoring, Modeling And Making Fantastic Families

Article # 14
Move Your Mornings
The top 3 ways to make your mornings move along

Ahhhh, yes. Another morning on it's way. You are out of the door, shirt untucked, papers falling out of your bag. One child is half in a coat, the other is screaming at you, though you are not quite sure what it was that you did NOW. Lunch for child number one (OH NO, DID YOU PACK THE KIDS LUNCH??? Oh, yes, yes, yes, yes.), consists of a squishy PB&J, almond butter of course (gotta be careful about those peanut allergies) and you are so happy that you remembered, THIS time, and some bag of something that you found in some drawer. The other? They got 20 bucks for a school lunch.

You're thinking, "How did I do this AGAIN, and why don't I have smaller bills to give to the kids? Well, that's $20 I'll never see again."

Swirling around your head are the questions, "Are mornings this crazy for everyone? Does everyone go to work as pissed off as I do? Does anyone really wake up and make their kids pancakes and eggs before school like on T.V.? Am I an awful parent?"

Banish those negative thoughts and mornings, in a few easy ways. Let's start with the thoughts.

- Yup, mornings are crazy for LOTS of people. You are not alone.
- Unfortunately many people go to work as frustrated as you. (Former teacher speaking here..... I have seen many drop offs

in my day and loads of parents are as flustered as you are in the morning.)

- Surely somewhere, someone is waking up and making pancakes and eggs before school. I have yet to meet them, but it is a big world so it must be happening somewhere.

NO, YOU ARE NOT AN AWEFUL PARENT!!!!!! You just are in need of a few new strategies and you are in luck because they are coming right up.

#1 Get Everything Ready For The Next Day Before Bedtime

A calm morning begins with an organized afternoon and evening. Getting just a few things done before bedtime, can make the next morning roll along without any (or many)bumps. Enlist the help of your kids to put their things in order for the next day. Even a 2,3,4,15,17 year old can help out.

Have your child pick out their outfit the night before, all the way down to socks, shoes, and accessories. If you have a child that is prone to changing their mind, allow for two outfits to be laid out and those are the ones that your child can choose from. No exceptions. It may be a struggle at first, but your child will hop on the bandwagon in a speedy way, especially if you give freedom to their choices. As long as it is weather appropriate, do you really care what they wear? The goal is to get out of the door on time or, gasp, early.

Put book bags, coats, boots and such in an easily accessible place and if possible, near the exit. This way as you are running out, no one is screaming about not being able to find their stuff. This goes for homework, hats, scarves, projects, even your briefcase or bag.

Make lunches. Older kids can pack their own (you can check them if you so wish) and younger kids can help or make theirs with your supervision. Just having the lunch packed and ready to go will save 10-15 minutes in the morning. Remember to put that lunchbox in the fridge the night before so in the morning, you can just grab and go.

There you are. Half of your morning is taken care of the night before. Your kids even did the bulk of it. NEXT.....

#2 Make A Homework Plan

How many times has your child left their homework for the morning or just forgot to do it? The crack of dawn, before going off to school is not the best time to finish things up. There are way too many goals on your list, to add homework as one of them.

Have a set homework time. Some kids need to wind down or play a bit when they get home, before they begin their homework. Other children need to do it right away or they are difficult to motivate. Work that out with your kids, but keep it consistent.

Homework does NOT have to be done in the same place all of the time. If your child finds it hard to sit in one spot, let them pick different places to do their homework. Writing may work at the table, but reading may be more comfy on the couch. As long as homework is finished and understood, let your kids have the choice of locations.

Dry erase calendars are good for multi-step assignments such as, reports or art projects. Dry erase boards will help your kids stay on track, and not leave bits of homework for the morning. Put each step that needs to be done and its due date on the calendar. For example:

- Monday: Read ten pages
- Tuesday: Read ten pages
- Wednesday: Read last ten pages
- Thursday: Outline book report and write rough draft
- Weekend: Finish report and put in bag (Notice, PUT IN BAG! After all of the work that your child has done, they will not want to leave it at home.)

Now your family has lunch packed, clothes out, bags and such by the door and homework finished. You have already bought yourself about 20-25 minutes. You might even have time to fully dress yourself before running out of the door. Onto the last idea. This one may be a toughie for some kids, and parents a like.

#3 Turn Off T.V. And Video Games In The A.M.

Children, and many grown ups for that matter, get very distracted by entertaining electronics. Once your child starts to watch a show or play a game, it may be very difficult (and cause time consuming arguments) when you try to tear them away. So what can you and your family do with all of that free time that you now have uncovered? Sleep, make pancakes and eggs (ha ha, just kidding), move slower?

Your child has now amassed so much time, even after taking care of their morning responsibilities (dressing, brushing teeth, eating breakfast) that they are now looking at you, scratch that, glaring at you because they are bored and you won't let them watch T.V. Give options to amuse your kids such as, reading a book or coloring. Ideas for activities that your child will not mind leaving and finishing later. Your older children are probably just fine texting their friends about how mean you are because you don't let them watch T.V. in the morning anymore. Whatever keeps 'em busy. You can also ask them what they would like to do, but stress that when it is time to go, it is time to go.

If your kid is all right leaving the T.V. or a video game, by all means, let your kid have at it. Many children do not have the ability to leave something so enticing once started.

Ahhhh, yes. Another morning on it's way. You are out of the door, shirt tucked, papers organized in your bag. Both kids in coats, walking quietly to the car or bus. Lunch is packed, mostly by your children. You smile as you imagine your little one eating their self-made turkey, pickle, and jelly sandwich. You also smile thinking about the $20 that you may spend on yourself that day. You're thinking, "I did it and I am soooooo treating myself to a $20 lunch."

Swirling around your head are the questions, "How did I ever survive mornings before? How can I help everyone go to work as relatively calm as I am? Does anyone really wake up and make their kids pancakes and eggs before school like on T.V. ? (O.K. That one still floors you.) Am I the best parent or what?". Congrats! You have now tackled one of the hardest parts of the day. MORNING. What's next? Perhaps world peace.

You think, "If I can bring peace to my morning, I can SURELY bring peace to the world. It will probably be much easier."

O.K. I'm A Parent, Now What?
Mentoring, Modeling And Making Fantastic Families

Article #15
It's All Fun And Games
Or
How to get through any situation without fighting with your kids

This is a little story about me and my two small friends out in the freezing cold, making a very bad situation into a fun adventure. You can do it too. You can make a bad situation fun and tantrum free. Yup, I do know how bold a statement that is, but read on and see how it is done so that you too can learn how games can make bad situations better.

OK, so let's set the scene. My friend had to work late and she asked me to pick up her boys (who I am very close to) from school and take them home for dinner. We both live in the city, so my plan was to bus it to the school, also in the city, and cab it back to their house for dinner. My friend had given me that suggestion because that is what seems to work best for them when a car-less parent does the pick up. So the day arrived and it, of course, turned out to be the coldest day of the winter AND the first snow. I am not sure what happens in your neck of the woods the first time it snows, but here, the world comes to a standstill and cars move like tired, old turtles. All of the business people, in their nice shoes and fancy clothes decide that cabs are the only way for them to get home. For them, their business attire and long walks to the bus stop will not mesh with the cold and snow. So it's a freezing, icy, traffic laden city and I am off to pick up the kids from school. I get there at 5, they go to an after school program and 5 is the pick up time, and that is when our adventure begins. The boys get all coat, hat and mittened up and we discuss the plan.

"OK boys here is the plan: We are going to head out in the cold. We need to look for a cab and then we will head home for dinner. You must hold my hands because it is very icy. Everyone ready?"

With a big "YES" we are on our way. We walk slowly and carefully to corner number one. We all stand quietly for a moment and begin to feel that maybe this is not the best spot to wait.

"Where do you stand when you get cabs with daddy?" I ask my five and a half year old friend. Yes, I just asked a five and a half year old where to catch a cab. Want to know why? Well, I'm gonna tell you. He catches a cab with his dad about 3 times a week and has been doing so for a year and a half. He knows a whole lot better then I do. I also know that putting him in charge of finding a cab makes him feel very important and will keep him from realizing how cold, tired and hungry he is.

He informs me of two spots. We head to spot number one, all the while I am yelping "Ok team, we have to keep our eyes pealed for a cab. Are your eyes pealed? We are on the job. We are on the look out. Who will be the one to find the cab?" Now even the 4 year old is into it. We are a team. We are in this together. It has been 15 minutes and we are getting cold. No cabs in site. Also, not one complaint, concern, or tantrum. We are all too busy on our hunt for a cab, stopping only to grumble emphatically when full ones pass us by.

"Oh my, another one full. Ug" We all complain in our own way. Consistently loud, cartoony and giggling.

As the minutes go by we get louder and more creative with our grumbles as if we are trying to out ridiculous each other. We talk about getting a plane or helicopter. We talk about being invisible. We talk about hopping on the top of a cab and riding it home.

It had been almost a half an hour. Yes, I said a half an hour with two kids under 6 in the cold after a long day of school and still not one complaint. Well, not a real one. Having had it myself, and feeling it was only a matter a time before these kids realize how not fun this all really is, I began to form a plan B. That is when I see a chain restaurant. I figure we can feed ourselves, waste some time and maybe find a cab once rush hour has slowed a bit. The boys agree that it is a good idea and we go in for a bite. When we sat at the table I thanked them for their patience and help and assured them that we would try again for round two after we eat. Dinner was lovely as we rehashed our adventure. I told the boys I was surely going to speak to their parents about their helpfulness and their super sleuthyness in our hunt for a cab. They loved THAT idea.

We finished up our yummy dinner and got pumped for Find A Cab Part Deux. We headed out all bundled up, and after about 10 more minutes, saw a cab down the block. We carefully ran in the silliest way that we knew how and jumped into the cab, thanking the driver again and again for waiting for us to get into the car. An act that takes a surprisingly long time when you have two kids all bundled up in big coats, hats, mittens, boots and the like, also lugging their backpacks. Then there was me, who was also all bundled, with my purse and a large bag of leftovers from dinner.

Once in the cab, the boys told the driver of our adventure, as if it were some great epic tale straight out of the Iliad. Once the story had been told, the boys settled into their seats and, with droopy eyes, and tried to explain how "exhausted" they were. At home they got into jammies and awaited their parents so they could retell the story of their great icy adventure.

You might be wondering why I am telling you all about this school pick up. Let me start by giving an alternative way the pick up could have gone:

I pick up the boys in a rush. Push them to get their coats on because I know how tired and hungry they are and they are not fun when they are tired and hungry. We have to hurry home before the inevitable meltdowns begin. "Let's go" I prod and I pull them out of the door of the school into the cold. "Hurry up. I have to find a cab." "Shhhh, don't talk to me now I'm thinking." "You're hungry? Well so am I. What do you what me to do about it? I don't have food in my pockets. We will be home soon. You can wait." I pull the kids all around trying different streets to find a cab all the while they whine and cry and at times refuse to move. They are a mess and so am I. We are freezing and hungry and tired and angry.

I tell you this story because more often then not, we grown ups forget that fun is vastly more motivating than yelling. No, really. It does not take much. Make a game out of whatever it is that you are doing. Perhaps you think making up a game takes too much energy. Energy that YOU do not have after a long day. I'll tell you this parents, it takes a lot less energy to make up a game, sing a song, and have fun with your kids, than it does to yell, rush and get angry. Finding a cab, getting dressed, brushing teeth; You can make a game out of almost any situation.

The next time you find yourself in an unpleasant pinch with your kids and you start to rush and pull and yell and snap, take a breath. Regroup and come together as a team to solve your crisis. Make a game out of it. Make it fun. Give everyone a job. Sing a song about what needs to be done. You will be surprised how much more pleasant those unpleasant situations will be and how much closer you will become with your children when you try to find the child in yourself. I'll tell you what. When I got home I kept thinking to myself how much more miserable I would have been in that situation if I were by myself, cold in the city trying to find a cab. Being with the kids made it much easier and more fun. When was the last time you said that to yourself? "Boy I am so glad that I have my kids here in the freezing cold, starving, tired and no cabs in sight." Or something of the sort. If you can't remember, than it's time to find the childlike adventurer in yourself and invite your kids to come along.

O.K. I'm A Parent, Now What?
Mentoring, Modeling And Making Fantastic Families

Article #16
Time Out Is Over And Out

"I said clean up the blocks or you get a time out!"

I know that "Time Out" is what adults are being told to tell non-listening children, but without explanation of why a child is in "Time Out" the life lesson is being lost. In the aforementioned scenario a child will hear this:

"I did not clean, so I am in trouble."

Maybe that IS what you are saying, but that will not prevent the mess leaving the next time your child is playing. If you choose "Time Out" as a consequence for your child, frame it so that it becomes a lesson instead of a punishment. So that, even if they are mad, children understand why they have to pause on playing or clean up their activity before moving on to another.

"I need you to clean up the blocks or you cannot move onto another activity. If you are not going to clean, you will have to stay here (yup this is the *Stuck* thing from Article #12) until you are ready. You choose when you get to move on." (Said in a calm, quiet voice.)

I am not saying you can't use the words "Time Out" if you so choose. I am just imploring you to use them clearly and with the intent of banishing the frustrating behavior, not the child.

O.K. I'm A Parent, Now What?
Mentoring, Modeling And Making Fantastic Families

O.K. I'm A Parent, Now What?
Mentoring, Modeling And Making Fantastic Families

Never fear spoiling children by making them too happy. Happiness is the atmosphere in which all good affections grow.

Anonymous

O.K. I'm A Parent, Now What?
Mentoring, Modeling And Making Fantastic Families

Article #17
Accentuate The Positive

"Don't touch that." "Don't run." "Don't yell" The word "Don't" is constantly being hurled at children in school, home, the bus, and everywhere for that matter. We have all used "Don't do..." and quite frankly we will again, to the dismay of kids everywhere. Now it is a time for clarity, creativity, and change. It's time to change our words from expressing what we don't want, to expressing what we do want. Instead of telling kids what NOT to do, try telling them what TO do. If you want your kids to stop yelling, tell them to use their inside or soft voices. If you want your kids to stop climbing on the furniture, let them know that feet stay on the floor. I know that I prefer to hear someone say,

"Please remove your shoes at the door." Instead of

"Don't walk in my house with shoes!"

When adults express what they expect, children have a clear picture of the behavior that is appropriate for that situation. The added bonus is that a child will feel empowered with important information, not punished by a quick reprimand.

O.K. I'm A Parent, Now What?
Mentoring, Modeling And Making Fantastic Families

Article #18
JUST GET DRESSED!!!!!!

or...

How To Get Out Of The House In The Morning On Time And With Your Sanity Intact

It is 7 am. Your hair is wet, you are half shaven, the coffee has yet to kick in, and the adorable little angel that you tucked in last night has transformed into a demanding, tearful, screaming, tantrum machine, all because you asked them to get dressed. They loved that outfit last week, but it becomes abundantly clear as it flies across the room that it is a favorite no more. An activity that should take 15 minutes has turned into a wet haired, pressure rising, yelling, hour and a half long struggle. Your child ends up being late to school and you, late to work. Your day is shot, but what is even worse is that today was not the first time that your morning has begun this way. This scene is now playing out all of the time. And about what?

CLOTHES!!!!

Ok, it is time to cool down, step back, and take a look at what is going on. As it has been said, "The definition of insanity is doing the same thing over and over and expecting different results." It is O.K. though. It happens to the best of us. We all find ourselves in a rut from time to time. Repeating the same action over and over and not knowing how to change our situation, but now it is time to turn a rut into a learning experience. A time to try something new. Here are some tips that may help you on your journey to a new, more enjoyable, morning adventure.

Your child has a need to feel in control of their lives.

By letting them control some of the smaller decisions in their lives, you will find the choice decisions being left to you.

Children enjoy expressing themselves with their clothing.

Oh, and yes I am talking about your 2, 3, 4, 5, 8, 11 year old. Is it really *THAT* big a deal if they think green stripes go with purple polka dots? The respect that you are giving them by letting them express themselves will be a strong foundation in the building of their sense of self and confidence.

You can give your child choices but still keep them weather appropriate.

Make seasonal drawers so that in the winter your child can only pick clothes from the "winter" drawers and they do not try to walk out of the door in a skirt and a tank top. Oh trust me; they will try to do that.

Here is a fun ditty that will help keep your kids focused and on track.

At night tell your child to "pick out your clothes from their head to your toes." This way your child will know what to expect in the morning. They will know that what is out to wear was their choosing. (And I am not kidding. Have your child pick out clothes all the way down to socks and shoes or there WILL be a battle over <u>THAT</u> in the morning.)

Most important of all is recognizing that your parenting skills are not reflected by your child's clothes matching, but instead, they are reflected by the skills and sense of self with which you send them off into the world. Watch as your child walks out of the house or into their classroom wearing brown sweatpants and a red and yellow sweater, or black pants and black shirt and black spiked hair and think to yourself, "**I am a GREAT parent!**" Oh feel free to allow yourself a little giggle when they are out of sight. I mean really. *They are wearing brown sweatpants with a red and yellow sweater.* What a great story for the office!!

O.K. I'm A Parent, Now What?
Mentoring, Modeling And Making Fantastic Families

Article #19
When "CAUSE I SAID SO!" Is Not Enough
A Plan For Creating Family Rules

Are your children confused about what is allowed and what is not allowed in your home? Do you and your partner have different ideas about what the kids can and cannot do? Is yelling the main form of communication in your world? Yes? This sounds like your family? Well, read on.

Clear rules are the key to a home that runs smoothly, at least most of the time. (Nothing runs smoothly ALL of the time.) When everyone in the family knows what is expected of them, they feel more comfortable and sure of the choices that they are expected to make. When rules are clear, there is no room left for all of the negotiating that is ardently utilized by children of all ages (as well as some grown ups I know).

Many families are unaware of the importance of clear and concise rules. Here are a few ideas on how to bring constructive rules into your home and foster the respect, teamwork, and fun that you and your family have been longing for:

- Sit down with your family, yup the kids too, and write down the rules that you *all* think will create a happy, safe, and respectful home. Including all of the family members will lay the groundwork for the teamwork mentioned earlier. You will be showing your children that they matter. That they are a vital and active part of the family. Not just young people who happen to live in the house.

- After writing everyone's ideas, cross out the ones you may not need (such as your three year olds suggestion of *no dinosaurs in the house*), and consolidate the others. Hitting, Kicking, and Pushing are all acts of aggression. Yelling, Teasing, and Ignoring are all acts of disrespect. They can each be combined into one word to keep things simple. By all means if your family needs the rules to be specific, go for it. You know your family and what will work for them. Watch out for too many rules though. They can get a bit overwhelming.

- The next step is to flip any negative rules into positive ones. Even we grown up people can get confused about what is expected of us when we are only told what <u>not</u> to do. Instead of telling your family what they cannot do, let them know what behaviors are desired. *No Hitting* turns into *Use kind and helping hands*. *No Yelling* turns into *Use calm, constructive communication*. *No Running* turns into *We use walking feet inside*.

- Here is the most important question for grown ups to ask themselves when making rules; Can YOU follow the rules?   YES YOU. THE GROWN UPS IN THE HOUSE. The rules that the family makes are for the family, **<u>the whole family</u>**. Yup, even you mom and dad. And even you grandma and grandpa. The rules are for EVERYONE in the house. If one rule is to *use kind hands* that means **you,** as the parents, need to use kind hands. If a rule is to *use quiet voices,* then **you** as the parents need to use quiet voices. (If you are yelling to keep a person from danger or are being silly and playing, yelling is just fine. Both are very good reasons to be loud.)

- Here is an example of a list of rules. Feel free to create your own. If you have a big place and don't mind running in the house. That is O.K. . If you have pets and want to add rules about them. GO FOR IT.

    1. We use kind and caring hands.
    2. We use our calm voices to solve disagreements.
    3. We use walking feet inside.
    4. We take responsibility for our actions.
    5. We treat each other the way we would like to be treated.

Wonderful, so now you have rules. I suggest no more than 5 to keep them easy to remember. Put them up where everyone can be reminded of them. Make the poster fun and attractive. These are positive affirmations that all members will need to be reminded of now and then. Yes, including the grown ups.

This may be a new take on rules for some. Most of us grew up with the "do nots" and the, "what not to do's". This is more about teaching your family what is expected of them, as opposed to what is not allowed. It is about learning and growing, not punishing.

Uh, oh. What's that? Oh. Someone broke a rule. What do you do then? Honestly, that is up to you. Some people do *time outs*, some take privileges away. While these may work in a sense, they do not create the learning experience that is so important for your child's development. The rules are there to instill important social behaviors that will be necessary throughout life. Grown ups can't have a tantrum because their proposal did not get picked. Well you can. We all know those people who do, but the outcome is never a positive one in the end.

So how do you make a poor choice into a great learning experience? When a child or grown up breaks a rule, they should be given a chance to make up for that action. (uh huh, I was serious. You want teamwork, you have to be part of the team.) The child or grown up needs to be given an opportunity to try again the "right" way. For example, if a child is using yelling words to get what they want, give them a gentle reminder. *"We use our calm words to solve problems."* Younger children may need to be given the words that you would like them to use. *Tell your sister, "I was not done with the car yet. Please give it back."*

Seems like more work you say? Well, at first, yes it is; but the payoffs are worth it. After a bit, the arguments about what is and is not allowed will end. The family will have learned that respect and kindness work better than yelling and hitting to get the desired effects. Children will learn that they are a valued part of the family. They will be more willing to help out the team when it is needed.

Excited? Ready for change? Got a pen and some paper? Maybe even glitter and stickers for the beautiful Family Rules poster?

Now gather everyone up, let the brainstorming begin, and watch your family grow together into a fun, respectful team.

O.K. I'm A Parent, Now What?
Mentoring, Modeling And Making Fantastic Families

Don't demand respect as a parent. Demand civility and insist on honesty. But respect is something you must earn -- with kids as well as with adults.

William Attwood

O.K. I'm A Parent, Now What?
Mentoring, Modeling And Making Fantastic Families

Article #20
Positive Parenting Philosophies

When a person thinks about creating a business they start with an idea such as, what will my business be? Then they may move onto a business plan. How will my business be run? What are my goals? What is the philosophy and feel of my company?

While, obviously, having children and parenting are not business endeavors, they do deserve and require the same kind of thought and planning that one would put into a business enterprise. Unfortunately when people make the life changing decision to have children they often end up winging it, feeling that they will figure it out along the way; That it just comes naturally. They have not sat down and discussed their parenting philosophies with each other. *How will we raise our children*, or *what does discipline means to us* are just two of the many important questions to be explored.

The family is the most important conglomerate that one will have in their lives. Remember parents, you and your partner are two different people with two different upbringings and possibly two different ideas on how to raise children. Coming up with a parenting philosophy will take time. That being said, how does one come up with a parenting philosophy? You can start by answering some thought provoking questions.

When you imagined parenthood, what did it look like?

Was it fun? Were the members of the family equals? Were there a firm set of rules to follow created by the parents? Was there a lot of communication between members or were children to follow the words of the grown ups in their lives? Did you eat meals together? Did you have help? A nanny or daycare? Did someone stay home, work flexible hours or part time? All that we imagine parenthood to be may not come true. Maybe a parent wants to be at home full time but money and the economy will not allow for that. If parents start with a utopian idea of what a family looks like to them, they can then try to create a reality that will hopefully come close to their vision.

As a parent what is your role?

Are you a maker of rules? Are you a friend? Are you a disciplinarian? Are you a protector? Are you the one who allows for struggles so as to learn? You can be different things at different times, but if you decide that you are usually the rule maker and sometimes friend then that lays a different groundwork than usually friend and sometime rule-maker. Will you be very involved in all aspects of your child's life? Will you coach every team? Be the driver to every event? Will your child find their own ways to their activities? Will your child depend on itself to navigate through their world?

When your children look back on their childhood what do you want them to think and feel about it?

First of all, is this statement a priority to you? Do you want your kids to feel that they had a happy childhood? A childhood full of strong foundations? A childhood that prepared them for the years to come? Do you want them to feel that their parents were always there? Will they remember parents who gave them room and independence? Will your children look back and remember anger or yelling? Not everyday will be filled with sunshine and fairy dust. Hard times do befall us all, but what overall view will your children have of their parents and childhood?

FOR THOSE WHO HAVE CHILDREN AND ARE NOW CREATING A POSITIVE PARENTING PHILOSOPHY.

If you were your child, how would your family feel and look to you?

Step into your children's shoes. Is your home a safe place, a place that you feel happy about being in? Do you have fun at home? Do you feel respected and heard? Do you want to be a member of your family? If you have teens or preteens, they may seem to want to be a whole separate entity. It may seem as if they do not want to be a part of your family at all. That is just the way it is supposed to be. They are flexing their grown up muscles, though small that they are. On the whole though, does your teen seem amused when with the family? Does your teen talk to you? Joke with you? Will your teen go on family outings and, though they may protest going, in the end have at least a bit of fun?

What lessons are you teaching your children?

Are your children learning to follow rules without question? Are you teaching your children to question authority respectfully when needed? Are your children learning that they are valued and must value others? Are your children learning that through fear and intimidation things get accomplished? Have your children learned that kindness is a resource? Will your children grow up feeling that violence is an acceptable way to solve problems? Will they be the ones being hurt? Are your children gaining the tools that they need to solve life's problems and conflicts?

When you imagined parenthood what did it look like?

Does your family resemble your hopes and ideas of family before kids? How does it differ from the life that you imagined? Are you satisfied with your family? Are you happy with your family? If not, what would you change? If so, what are those things that make you happy and satisfied? How will you keep them going?

Parenting Philosophies will change over time as children and parents grow, learn, and experience life. There will be times when your family is strolling right down the road that you imagined and at other times your family may feel lost and distant. Your parenting philosophy is a place to come back to when the family has lost its way; A place to regroup and find your path again. A place to remind you of what is really important to you. Take some time, and please do give yourself time, to explore these questions and create your own Parenting Philosophy and lay your family's path.

Article # 21
Logical Consequences; A Parents Best Friend

There are many discipline and punishment techniques that parents impart on their kids in order to get them to listen, follow directions, or mold them into "good" people. Some popular methods are time out, yelling, taking away toys or T.V., and grounding, just to name a few. An interesting tidbit about all of the aforementioned reactions is that many parents find that they have to implement them over and over again. If you have to implement your punishments or disciplines over and over and over again, then they are not working and it is time to move on. Move on to what??? You might be thinking. Move on to what works best. Logical consequences and taking responsibility for ones actions.

In many homes a child who spills paint on the floor because they are being a bit too wild at the paint table is put in time out while a parent cleans the mess. A child yells at mom and so she takes away his T.V. time that week. A child hits their brother and the parents have that child miss baseball practice. A child does not eat all of their lunch, so they cannot play outside. Sure, these are some popular ways to discipline in these situations, but they are not the most effective.

So if the above consequences are not the best way to handle disciplinary situations, what is? Finding suitable discipline is all about having children remedy and take care of a situation that they caused or have a consequence that has to do with their negative action. "HUH?", You are thinking. "Sure it is easy to think about those types of consequences in hindsight." True, coming up with a logical consequence on the spot can be tough at first, AT FIRST. After a little practice, it becomes a lot easier. Let's take a closer look at the situations mentioned above.

The Playing Paint Spiller

This child was bouncing and playing and not sitting or standing calmly while using paint. Because of all of the bouncing, the paint spilled. First, as grown ups, we have to be proactive. Do not have kids use paint on carpets or near anything that you do not want getting dirty. You want to make sure that you are not setting your kids up to fail. I am a grown up and when I paint, I make a mess. How can I expect a child to keep things clean when I have a hard time doing so myself? After thinking proactively and making sure that your child is not on carpet or near anything of value, you may find that your stress about mess has diminished a tad.

All may go well for a bit, but then you notice that your sweet child has ants in their paints, here is where the logical consequence thought process begins. Take a look at the situation and what may happen. You see the possibility of paint on the floor because your child will not sit at the paint table. If a child cannot follow the rules of the paint table what needs to happen? The paint goes away for the day. (Some schools say that the activity is closed. It is a good idea to brush up on your child's school lingo for clearer communication.)

Perhaps you were busy and missed seeing him get bouncy again. You missed the opportunity to watch the blue paint topple off of the table onto the floor. Take a breath, think clearly and say to yourself, "What needs to happen if the paint spills on the floor? It needs to be cleaned up." As much as you might be tempted to clean the mess yourself and throw your child into time out, don't. The idea here is to impart Logical Consequences as the discipline. That being said, who do you think should be cleaning up the mess?

You might be thinking at this point. "Have my child clean up paint? That is ridiculous. It would make a bigger mess."

Your child does not have to clean up all of it. Perhaps they can help you clean the paint or they can clean a bit and then you take over. The idea is to have your child learn something from their mistake: When I make a mess I need to clean it up. When I do not use my paint the right way it goes away. I need to sit or stand calmly at the paint table if I want to use the paint.

Just a wee FIY here; Your child may be less than thrilled at the prospect of the paint going away. That is OK. They may cry or have a tantrum. Again, that is OK. We all get upset when things do not go our way. Some kids have no reaction and may not seem to be upset at all. On these occasions a parent might feel that they should be tougher. They feel that unless a child is upset, the discipline is not working. Discipline is not about making a child cry, but about teaching a life lesson. Your child has learned that when they make a mess they must clean it up and when they do not follow the rules of a play area, that play area gets shut down or those activities get put away. Those are lessons to be carried through a lifetime.

The Yeller

Our next friend is one who tends to express themselves and their dissatisfaction through yelling at those around them. "I HATE PANCAKES. I DO NOT WANT PANCAKES. MAKE ME

SOMETHING ELSE." "I AM NOT GOING TO BED. I HATE YOU. NO. NO. I AM NOT DONE WATCHING TELEVISION"

Again, be proactive. Think of yourself as a super sleuth. Nancy Drew, Sherlock Holmes, (insert your favorite detective here). What seems to set your child off? What do they look or act like before they start yelling? It is much easier to talk to a person who has not yet hit the roof and lost the ability to be rational, than one in tantrum mode. At the point where they look like they are beginning to get upset or when you stumble upon a situation that you know upsets them, try to come up with a solution to solve the problem at hand before the yelling begins.

Parent, "You look upset. What can you do to feel better (or what can you do to fix the problem...)

If your child has passed calm and rational, and is at destination yelling, stay calm and think logically. What would be a logical consequence for someone who is yelling? What would you do if a grown up was yelling at you and you did not want to fight? One choice is to walk away or excuse the yeller (excusing a child tends to be a bit more difficult, but if your child responds, tell them the places in the house that they can go and yell. Their room for example.) Let your child know that you would like to hear them, but you do not want to be yelled at. Until they can talk calmly they need to excuse themselves or you will excuse yourself, and others in the room. If you have a very young child you can move to another part of the room and sit quietly until the episode has ended. We don't want to put kids in an unsafe situation. Also remember that discipline is about life lessons. Children (and some adults) need to learn how to express their emotions positively. If a child has a difficult time expressing anger, they do not need more anger being thrown at them.

They need to learn how to productively express their ideas and feelings.

Example: Parent, "You sound very upset about your homework. Homework can be frustrating." Leave it at that for a moment and see what they say. Give time for your child to think. The silence can be hard but hang in there. "I hear your words but I cannot understand you when you are yelling. I also do not like to be yelled at. If you want to talk to me I will listen, but if you continue to yell at me because I will not do your homework for you, I will walk away." "You are continuing to yell at me. If you want my help you can ask me for help, but right now I am going to go into the living room. When you are ready to use your calm words, I will be ready to listen."

"BUT WHAT ABOUT WHEN THEY FOLLOW? MY KIDS ALWAYS FOLLOW ME???"

(You might be thinking.)

That can be a tough one. You do not want to play chase all over the house or lock your child in or out of rooms. If your child follows you, have a seat and sit quietly. No matter what your child does to get your attention, do not respond until they are calm. You have explained how you would like them to communicate and until they follow the directions, stay calm and quiet. If your child asks why you are not talking respond by asking, "You tell me why I am not talking?" Be careful not to use a sarcastic or harsh tone when you ask. The reason for the question is so that your child can stop and think about the situation at hand and realize that you are not talking because they are yelling. If the child wants you to talk, they must stop yelling. When children have to answer questions about a situation that involves them, it really drives the point home.

As mentioned, the logical consequence of someone yelling at you is for you to walk away, but the lesson does not stop there. Your children still needs to learn how to express themselves in a productive manner and why it was that their behavior was not acceptable. At a calm moment, talk to your child about what happened and teach your child how they should speak to you when they are upset.

Parent to child, "Earlier you were very upset and that is all right. What was not all right was you yelling at me. If you are upset you can say, "I am really mad that I have to go to bed. I am not ready. I am mad at you for making me go to bed." I do not mind you being upset with me, but I do mind the yelling". (Remember that you must model the behavior that you want to see in and from your children. If you do not want them to yell, then you must not yell.)

Now that some behaviors and consequences have been put forth, it is time to practice. You will see a behavior then you will fill in the logical consequence and why that is a logical consequence. When you have finished head to: www.OkImAParent.com to find ideas to go with the presented scenarios.

Behavior: Child hits sibling or friend:

Logical Consequence:

_____

_____

Why:
_____

_____

Behavior: Child will not eat their meal:

Logical Consequence:
_____

_____

Why:
_____

_____

Behavior: Child draws on the wall:

Logical Consequence:
_____

_____

Why:
_____

_____

Behavior: Child comes home late from practice or a friends house:

Logical Consequence:
_____

_____

Why:
_____
_____

Behavior: Your scenario:
_____
_____

Logical Consequence:
_____
_____

Why:
_____
_____

Final Thoughts...

Parents, you are the greatest and most influential educational tools that your children are exposed to and experience. You are the people that your children will behold and mirror. When parents model positive behaviors, their children will emulate those positive behaviors. When parents model negative behaviors, their children will emulate those negative behaviors. Children get their social cues from you. Be sure to display the cues with which you would like your children to go out into the world and display. Most importantly, when children are respected and treated as the independent human beings that they are, they will be happier, empowered, and become more cooperative. By incorporating the strategies that you have discovered in this book, you will experience family transformations that you had never thought possible.

I invite you to end your journey with the same powerful words that you began with:

Your children will become what you are; so be what you want them to be.

David Bly

Recommended Reading

Recommendations for both children and parents

For Kids

Get Ready For Baby
Alexander, Martha G. (1979). *When the New Baby Comes, I'm Moving Out*. New York: The Dial Press
Corey, Dorothy (1992*)*. *Will There Be A Lap For Me?*. Illinois: Whitman, Albert & Company
Sheldon, Annette (2005). *Big Sister Now*. Washington, DC: Magination Press

Feelings
Aliki (1984). *Feelings*. New York: Greenwillow Books
Bang, Molly (1999). *When Sophi Gets Angry --- Really, Really Angry*. New York: Blue Sky Press
Curtis, Jamie Lee (1998). *Today I Feel Silly*. New York: HarperCollinsPublishers
Dr. Seuss (1996). *My Many Colored Days*. New York: Knopf
Parr, Todd (2005). *The Feelings Book*. New York: LB Kids

Death And Dying
Buscaglia, Leo (1982). *The Fall Of Freddie the Leaf*. New York, N.Y. : Distributed to the trade by Holt, Rinehart and Winston
De Paola, Tomie (1973). *Nana Upstairs & Nana Downstairs*. New York: Putnam's

Mellonie, Bryan (1983). *Lifetimes: The Beautiful Way to Explain Death to Children.* New York: Bantam Books
Viorst, Judith (1971). *Tenth Good Thing About Barney.* New York, N.Y.: Atheneum Books for Young Readers

For Parents

Parenting

Faber, Adele and Elaine Mazlish (1980). *How To Talk So Kids Will Listen & Listen So Kids Will Talk.* New York: Perennial Currents

Ginott, Haim (1965). *Between Parent And Child.* New York, Macmillan

Hart, Sura (2006). *Respectful Parents, Respectful Kids.* CA: PuddleDancer Press

Kurcinka, Mary Sheedy (2000). *Kids, Parents, and Power Struggles.* New York: HarperCollins Publishers

Kurcinka, Mary Sheedy (2006). *Raising Your Spirited Child.* New York: Harper

Pipher, Mary (1994). *Reviving Ophelia: Saving the Selves of Adolescent Girls.* New York: Ballantine Books

Turecki, Stanley (1995). *Normal Children Have Problems Too.* New York: Bantam Books

www.ingramcontent.com/pod-product-compliance
Lightning Source LLC
Chambersburg PA
CBHW031649040426
42453CB00006B/251